AF481160

Elliott is getting ready to explore.
He's going somewhere he has not been before.
Soon he will get the chance to embark...
On an adventure to Acadia National Park.

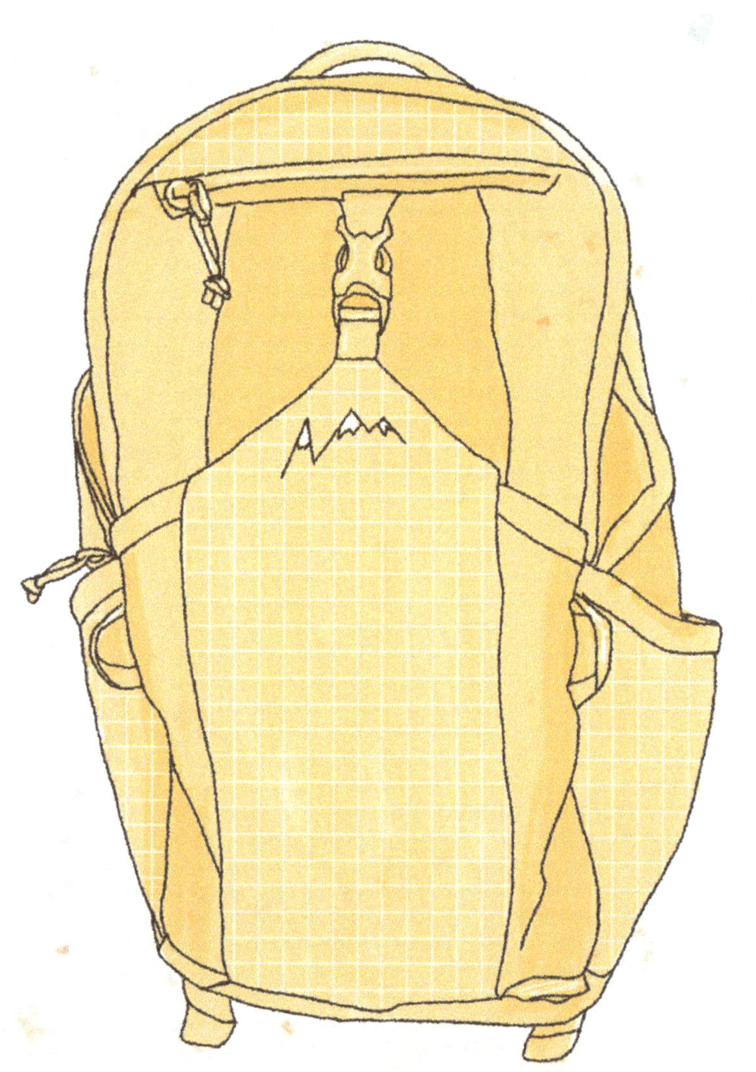

First, he needs
his pack.
This is the pack
he wears on
his back.
What should
Elliott put in
his pack...
this pack that
he wears on
his back?

Will he need a snack?
Will he need his map?

Will he need his red first aid kit he got from his Pap?
What about his fish Jack?
Hm, I don't know about that.

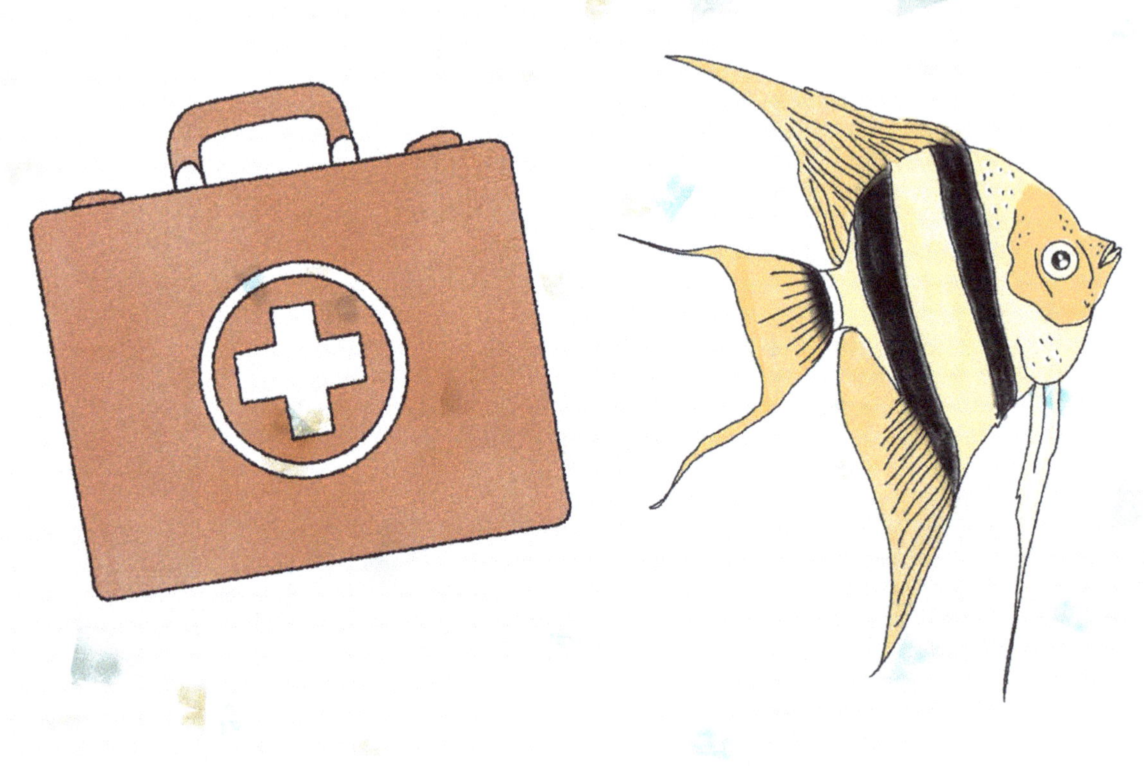

Will he need his sunscreen?
Will he need his compass that's green?

Will he need his water canteen?
What about his new gumball machine?

Will he need his binoculars that help him see far away?
Will he need his sunglasses to shade his
eyes throughout the day?

Will he need his bug spray that
helps keep the bugs at bay?
What about his rock collection?
Would that be okay?

Will he need his flashlight that helps him see at night?
Will he need his raincoat that packs up small and tight?

What about
his kite that
loves to
take flight?
I don't
think that
will fit
quite right.

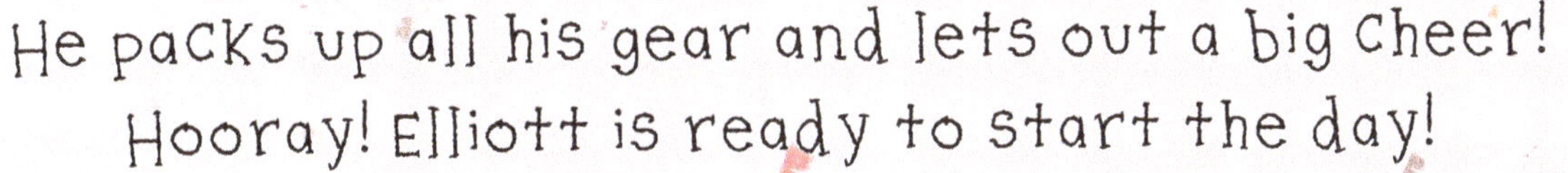

He packs up all his gear and lets out a big cheer!
Hooray! Elliott is ready to start the day!

After a long drive, they finally arrive,
and decide to hike a trail called The Beehive.

Next, they visit Thunder Hole.
The waves here are big and beautiful.
But watch your step as you stroll
the rocks are slippery so be careful!

Elliott and his family are so fond of this park, they decide to stay at Jordan Pond until it gets dark.

Elliott has so much fun exploring,
as soon as he gets back in the car, he's snoring.

He dreams of all the things
he's seen, like trees,
mountains, waves
and streams...

...and loons, lobsters, beavers
and otters, all swimming around
in Coastal waters...

...and bleeding tooth mushrooms,
rose root flowers and dragonflies
zooming around for hours.

When he wakes
up, he's ready
for more.
I wonder where
Elliott will go
next to
explore?